Fat Chance

Why Pigs Will Fly Before America
Has an Atheist President

Ray Comfort

First printing: June 2016

New Leaf Press, P.O. Box 726, Green Forest, AR 72638

New Leaf Press is a division of the New Leaf Publishing Group, Inc.

ISBN: 978-0-89221-745-8
Library of Congress Number: 2016940760

Cover image Shutterstock.com; cover caricatures by Esly Carrero (www.esly.net)
Edited by Lynn Copeland

Please consider requesting that a copy of this volume be purchased by your local library system.

Printed in the United States of America

Please visit our website for other great titles:
www.newleafpress.net

For information regarding author interviews, please contact the publicity department at (870) 438-5288.

New Leaf Press
A Division of New Leaf Publishing Group
www.newleafpress.net

Contents

Chapter One

Why Are There No Atheists in Congress?

American Atheists, Inc., the group founded by notorious activist Madalyn Murray O'Hair, boldly (and incorrectly) claims there are 35 million atheists in America. That number is highly exaggerated, as we will see; still, if there were even a third of that figure, most atheists must wonder why there isn't one fellow nonbeliever serving on Capitol Hill today. Some would argue that there has been one avowed atheist: Rep. Pete Stark. But after admitting his atheism, his support began to tumble. He was able to defeat one Democratic challenger, then lost the next election to a Christian:

> So far, only one sitting congressman, Pete Stark of California, has ever admitted to being an atheist while in office. First elected in

1972, Stark came out of the atheist closet back in 2007, but he lost his re-election bid in 2012 after serving in the U.S. House for 40 years.[1]

In a *Huffington Post* article titled "Here Are All the Atheists in Congress," another congressman was said to be an atheist, who "came out" after his retirement in 2013:

> A few months after retiring, former Rep. Barney Frank (D-Mass.) also announced his nonbeliever status, a declaration he made more than 25 years after coming out as the first openly gay member of Congress. That Frank felt more comfortable going public with his sexuality in 1987 than he did with his secular beliefs at any point during his House career says a lot about the stigma surrounding atheism in electoral politics.[2]

However, in his memoir, published in 2015, Rep. Frank corrected that misunderstanding and refuted the atheist label:

> Subsequently, after leaving office, I half-jokingly objected when Bill Maher, one of my favorite TV hosts, asked if I felt uncomfortable sitting next to a pot-smoking atheist on the set of his show. I replied that there were two of us on that stage who fit those categories. The media reached the conclusion that I had come out as an atheist. *In fact, I am not an atheist.* I don't know enough to have any firm view on the subject, and it has never seemed important to me. I have had a life-long aversion to wrestling with questions that I know I can

never answer. My tolerance for intellectual uncertainty is very low.[3]

But what about Vermont Senator Bernie Sanders, a socialist and 2016 Democratic presidential candidate? Some atheists are hopeful that one of their own could end up in the White House even this year. Of the four most likely candidates at this point, outspoken evangelical Ted Cruz is a Southern Baptist, Donald Trump grew up Presbyterian, and Hillary Clinton identifies as a Methodist. But CelebAtheists.com has a listing for Sanders and asserts "Bernie indicates he doesn't believe in God":

> Larry Sanders sums up his brother's views this way: "He is quite substantially not religious."... In October of 2015 Bernie Sanders was on Jimmy Kimmel live. Bernie didn't profess a theistic belief, indicated he didn't believe in god, and promoted the ideals [of] humanism.... Jimmy Kimmel says "A moment ago you said God forbid, you say you're culturally Jewish, *do you believe in god? Bernie instantly says, 'No'* while Jimmy is mid-sentence."[4] (emphasis in original)

The website lists him under "Ambiguous." I find that listing a God-believer as "Ambiguous" on Celeb Atheists is like listing Hillary Clinton on Celeb Republicans. But more importantly, Sanders did not say "No." According to *The Washington Post*:

> When late-night TV host Jimmy Kimmel asked Sanders in October whether he believes in God and if that matters to the American people, the senator seemed to avoid a direct

response: "I am what I am," he said. "And what I believe in, and what my spirituality is about, is that we're all in this together."[5]

In an article titled "Bernie Sanders disappoints some atheists with his 'very strong religious' feelings," the writer stated,

> Presidential hopeful Bernie Sanders dashed the hopes of some atheists when he declared he had "very strong religious and spiritual feelings" at a Democratic town hall. "It's a guiding principle in my life, absolutely, it is," Sanders said Wednesday (Feb. 3) when a New Hampshire voter asked him about his faith. "Everybody practices religion in a different way. To me, I would not be here tonight, I would not be running for president of the United States, if I did not have very strong religious and spiritual feelings." The statement came a week after the Vermont senator told *The Washington Post* he is "not active in any organized religion" but believes in God.[6]

This is consistent with what he said in a November 2015 interview with *Rolling Stone*. After noting that he had a Jewish upbringing but was not observant, he was asked directly, "Do you believe in God?" Sanders replied, "Yeah, I do. I do."[7]

Jack Jenkins, Senior Religion Reporter for Think Progress, acknowledges,

> Outside of prominent roles in television or the music industry, being elected to national office is often one of the most visible steps

a minority group can take to win acceptance in American society. Yet, for the millions of Americans who openly identify as atheist, the goal of political representation currently remains just out of reach: At present, no one in the 113th Congress identifies as an atheist.[8]

The same remains true of the 114th Congress. Gary Scott Smith, writing in *The Washington Post*, agrees that Congress remains out of reach for nonbelievers: "Being identified as an atheist in the United States today is still such a major political liability that a candidate holding this position probably could not gain a major party's nomination for president or even the Senate."[9] Jack Jenkins offered his thoughts on why atheistic views aren't likely to be heard in the halls of Congress:

> The most practical reason for the lack of atheists in Congress is that, generally speaking, unbelief polls pretty terribly with the American people. A Pew Research survey conducted in May found that Americans consider atheism the least attractive trait for a candidate to possess, with voters more likely to back a candidate who smokes marijuana, has never held office, or has had an extramarital affair than a self-professed atheist.[10]

In an article titled "Americans are deeply religious, so will we ever see an atheist president?" Gary Scott Smith elaborates on the difficulty of an atheist being elected:

> In numerous surveys, at least half of Americans state that they would not vote for

an atheist. While the numbers of those who declare that they would not vote for an atheist have declined in the new millennium, a 2014 Pew Research Center poll found that Americans are less likely to vote for an atheist than any other type of candidate. . . .[11]

Then he puts his finger on why ham will be flying over the White House roof before an atheist will be elected president:

> First, many Americans perceive atheists to be untrustworthy, insensitive and morally rootless. Despite their recent campaign to improve their image, a 2014 Pew poll found that Americans rated atheists more unfavorably than any religious group including Muslims. Second, in other polls, most respondents (as many as 72 percent) said they want the president to have strong religious beliefs. Many Americans also say they want presidents to seek God's guidance about the major decisions they must inevitably make.[12]

Hans Villarica, writing in *The Atlantic*, reported on a study that concluded atheists were as trustworthy as rapists:

> Distrust, not disgust, is the motivation behind believers' antipathy against atheists. In one of the six trials, participants found a description of an untrustworthy person to be more representative of atheists than of Christians, Muslims, gay men, feminists, or Jewish people. Only rapists were distrusted to a similar degree.[13]

Distrust of atheists isn't confined to American culture. A 2015 study in the United Kingdom found that people's distrust of atheists is deeply ingrained, *"with even many atheists having an instinctual distrust of each other."*[14] Another study asked participants to choose between an atheist and a religious candidate for a job. For a high-trust job such as daycare workers, people were much more likely to prefer the religious candidate over the atheist. The results of this study were reported in a *Scientific American* article titled "In Atheists We Distrust," in which the author wrote,

> It wasn't just the highly religious participants who expressed a distrust of atheists. People identifying themselves as having no religious affiliation held similar opinions. [Researcher] Gervais and his colleagues discovered that people distrust atheists because of the belief that people behave better when they think that God is watching over them. This belief may have some truth to it. . . . When we know that somebody believes in the possibility of divine punishment, we seem to assume they are less likely to do something unethical.[15]

Why would the average American prefer an inexperienced, dope-smoking adulterer to lead the country, rather than an atheist? There are three primary reasons.

The First Reason

If an individual knows that God sees him and will subject him to divine punishment, he can be more trusted to do what is morally right. While the words

"God-fearing" are often maligned, we know that if a man truly fears God he won't lie to you, steal from you, or kill you. This is because he has the biblical promise that His Creator will hold him accountable for how he treats others.

Atheists, of course, don't believe that God sees them and have no fear of judgment for any "bad" behavior. Their code of ethics is that morality is determined on earth, not in heaven. Because they believe there are no moral absolutes, which are true for all people in all times, their ethics can vary from one place to another and from one year to the next. If society says that something is morally sound today, then it becomes morally sound for them. Many have no solid moral code when it comes to lying, stealing, adultery, fornication, blasphemy, abortion, homosexuality — and even pedophilia. High-profile atheist Richard Dawkins, for example, doesn't condemn what he calls "just mild touching up":

> I am very conscious that you can't condemn people of an earlier era by the standards of ours. Just as we don't look back at the 18th and 19th centuries and condemn people for racism in the same way as we would condemn a modern person for racism, I look back a few decades to my childhood and see things like caning, like mild pedophilia, and can't find it in me to condemn it by the same standards as I or anyone would today.[16]

How could anyone so lack a fear of God that he could condone the sexual abuse of children in any era? Those who have no fear of judgment by a holy God can also easily justify "fibbing" if it suits their needs. During the

2016 presidential race, for example, America Atheists, Inc., stretched the truth about how many atheists are in the United States. They tweeted a meme in which they pictured Senator Marco Rubio saying, "America does not make sense unless we believe in a Creator." Under his words they added, "Speak for yourself. 35 million American atheists."[17]

In other words, Americans who profess atheism are presumably a powerful political voice. The problem is that there aren't anywhere near 35 million atheists in the United States. Pew Research Center's 2014 Religious Landscape Study found that just 3.1 percent of American adults described themselves as atheists when asked about their religious identity.[18] That translates to fewer than 10 million people.

But adding more than 25 million to the figure is no big deal when you don't believe in moral absolutes. Others cite even more extravagant figures. Writing in *The Washington Post*, Gregory Paul and Phil Zuckerman claim, "Surveys designed to overcome the understandable reluctance to admit atheism have found that as many as 60 million Americans — a fifth of the population — are not believers."[19]

David Silverman, president of American Atheists, Inc., has also been accused of intentionally stretching the truth. Describing Silverman's statements on a CNN special titled "Atheists: Inside the World of True Nonbelievers" (airing March 23, 2015), a Duke University researcher wrote:

> During the program, Silverman made a few factual errors that should bother even the most ardent atheist. Early on, he said that one in three Americans under the age of 30 is an atheist, but even under the loosest, most

awkward definition of an atheist (someone who doesn't believe in any god or gods), the actual number is off quite a bit. Thirty-two percent of millennials are *unaffiliated*, meaning they say they don't belong to any particular religious group. That doesn't make them atheists, though — 86 percent of unaffiliated millennials say they believe in God, meaning only about 5 percent of millennials are atheists (though, according to Pew, only 3 percent identify as such). It's understandable to make this slip-up once or twice, but Silverman has been corrected on this basic oversight for about four years. After so long, it's hard not to suspect that the mistake is calculated.[20]

Past Generations and Atheists

Neither have atheists been trusted by past generations, which have deemed atheists unfit for the White House since our nation's founding. It must be remembered that most of America's founders believed in God and the Bible. As they relied on God in forming this great nation, they expected its officials to continue to rely on God for wisdom to lead it. Even today, the president is sworn in by raising his right hand toward heaven and placing his left hand on a Bible while taking the oath of office, typically ending "So help me God."

James Madison, integral in the drafting of the Constitution and the Bill of Rights, declared in 1785:

> Before any man can be considered as a member of Civil Society, he must be considered as a subject of the Governor of the Universe. . . .[21]

If submission to God was necessary to be considered a good citizen, how much more to be a good president? John Witherspoon, who signed the Declaration, believed atheists were therefore not qualified for office:

> He is the best friend to American liberty who is the most sincere and active in promoting true and undefiled religion, and who sets himself with the greatest firmness to bear down profanity and immorality of every kind. *Whoever is an avowed enemy of God, I scruple not to call him an enemy to his country.*[22]

Lest any think this is discrimination that would be deemed "unconstitutional" today, it certainly was not to the men who wrote the Constitution. John Jay, one of the Founding Fathers and the first Chief Justice of the U.S. Supreme Court, was even more direct. He wrote in 1816: "Providence has given to our people the choice of their rulers, and it is the duty as well as the privilege and interest of our Christian nation to select and prefer Christians for their rulers."[23]

Founding Father Noah Webster summarized what he and many others — from our nation's birth to today — would consider the qualifications for the president of the United States:

> It is alleged by men of loose principles, or defective views of the subject, that religion and morality are not necessary or important qualifications for political stations. But the Scriptures teach a different doctrine. They direct that rulers should be men who rule in the fear of God, able men, such as fear God, men of truth, hating covetousness. . . .

When a citizen gives his vote to a man of known immorality, he abuses his civic responsibility; he sacrifices not only his own interest, but that of his neighbor; he betrays the interest of his country.[24]

So one reason atheists are rejected as political candidates is that they are deemed untrustworthy, because they have no fear of God. In the next chapter we will look at the second reason there are no atheists in Congress.

Chapter Two

Why Are Atheists so Vilified?

In a 2014 Pew Research survey, the vast majority of Americans —a whopping 89 percent — reported that they believe in God.[25] That translates to close to 284 million people. So it would be safe to say that there are over 200 million Americans who believe in God and country, celebrate Christmas and Easter, or Hanukkah, believe in the Ten Commandments, thank God at Thanksgiving, attend church or synagogue regularly, own a Bible, sing "God Bless America" (and mean it), and pray at night. They appreciate their freedom of religion, and so they count these things as being sacred.

With those thoughts in mind, let's look at the second reason there are presently no atheists sitting in Congress.

Run your eyes over the following sampling of highly publicized lawsuits. Please don't skim over this list. Take the time to think about each one — who it is that atheists are suing and the crime that was allegedly committed:

- Atheists sue to get prayer and God out of presidential inauguration[26]
- Atheists sue to remove "In God We Trust" from money[27]
- Atheist group threatens suit over "angels" on teacher's memorial[28]
- Atheists sue IRS over "Pulpit Freedom Sunday"[29]
- Atheist sues Navy for rejection as chaplain[30]
- Atheist groups sue to remove clergy housing exemption[31]
- Atheists sue after child "exposed" to cross on field trip permission slip[32]
- Atheists sue county in fight over marriage registers[33]
- Atheists sue regarding Ten Commandments on church land[34]
- Atheists sue over cross in World Trade Center museum[35]
- Atheists sue Texas governor over Capitol nativity display[36]
- Atheists stop Bible readings, remove posters from Alabama school[37]
- Florida sheriff to keep preaching in uniform despite atheist threats[38]
- Atheist move halts Christmas tradition in Santa Monica[39]
- Atheist Grinches sue Indiana schools over nativity scene[40]

- Atheists force Minnesota town to pull nativity scene[41]
- Atheists demand removal of biblical scenes in school Christmas play[42]
- Atheists sue Franklin County over nativity on courthouse grounds[43]
- Atheists sue Florida mayor over prayer vigil[44]
- Atheists demand town remove Christmas displays[45]
- Atheists use children to bash Christmas in billboard campaign[46]
- Atheist threatens suit over Corpus Christi cross planned for church property[47]
- Atheist group threatens to sue principal for praying[48]
- Atheists sue to stop Indiana school's live nativity scene[49]
- Florida atheists sue to silence prayers at Lakeland city meetings[50]
- Arkansas atheists sue over bus ads on God-free lifestyle[51]
- School cancels toy drive for the poor after atheists threaten to sue[52]
- Atheist threatens to sue for right to perform weddings in Vegas[53]
- Atheists win suit to ban FL school football team chaplain[54]
- Atheists threaten to sue over discount for praying before meals[55]
- Atheist group sues Texas sheriff over cross decals[56]

- Atheists sue Morris County, NJ, over Historic Preservation grants to churches[57]
- Atheists sue to include nontheistic messages in Brevard County, FL, meetings[58]
- Atheists sue over school board prayer in Chino Valley, CA[59]
- Atheist lawsuit seeks removal of Pennsylvania Ten Commandments[60]
- Atheists sue for the removal of Oklahoma Ten Commandments[61]
- Atheists sue to remove Florida Ten Commandments[62]
- Atheist parolee, forced into religious drug treatment program, wins almost $2 million in lawsuit[63]
- Teen atheist wins lawsuit to remove school religious banner[64]
- Atheist group sues to remove Peace Cross, a WWI memorial[65]
- Atheists win suit to declare Secular Humanism a religion[66]
- Atheist sues to ban Colorado Day of Prayer proclamation[67]
- Atheist group threatens restaurant over church discount[68]
- Atheist wins lawsuit prohibiting Gideon Bible handouts in Indiana schools[69]
- Atheists sue over Christmas toy drive on Air Force base[70]
- Atheist wins suit against Pittsburgh over bus ads[71]

- Atheists sue Kentucky city to remove cross from water tower[72]
- Atheists successfully sue Pismo Beach council over prayers[73]
- Atheists sue over painting of Jesus in Ohio school[74]
- Atheists win suit to prevent Christian group from meeting in school[75]
- Atheists win lawsuit against Green Bay crèche[76]
- Atheists win suit declaring Wisconsin's Good Friday legal holiday "unconstitutional"[77]
- Atheists force mayor to disclaim "Day of Prayer"[78]
- Atheists allege "culture of religion" at Ohio school[79]
- Atheists halt Michigan public school team prayer[80]
- Atheist sues Christian business for "religious" accommodation[81]
- Atheists sue Texas county over crosses on vehicles[82]
- Atheists sue to edit Pledge of Allegiance in NJ school[83]
- Atheists sue over Pennsylvania bus ads[84]
- Atheist group awarded $22,500 in lawsuit over Georgia coach-led-prayer[85]
- Atheists sue to stop Christian groups from helping ex-cons[86]
- Atheists sue every retail store in mall over "Happy Holidays"[87]

This is by no means an exhaustive list, and the majority of these cases occurred just in the last three years.

Atheists are suing their fellow Americans for things they hold dear, and it's all done under the guise of loving the Constitution. Most Americans believe we were created by God with certain unalienable rights — life, liberty, and the pursuit of happiness — and that our freedoms come from God, not from the government. Yet atheists are attempting to take away our most precious freedom — the freedom of religion — through an abuse of the court system. Despite the First Amendment's Establishment Clause, which says "Congress shall make no law respecting an establishment of religion, or *prohibiting the free exercise thereof*," atheists are trying to turn it into government-sanctioned hostility toward religion.

The continual media reporting of this constant barrage of atheist lawsuits has created an understandable resentment toward these people. Given all these attempts to strip away our religious freedoms, the public perception of nonbelievers is not surprising:

> Long after blacks and Jews have made great strides, and even as homosexuals gain respect, acceptance and new rights, there is still a group that lots of Americans just don't like much: atheists. Those who don't believe in God are widely considered to be immoral, wicked and angry. . . . Surveys find that most Americans refuse or are reluctant to marry or vote for nontheists; in other words, nonbelievers are one minority still commonly denied in practical terms the right to assume office despite the constitutional ban on religious tests.[88]

Yet the irony is that atheists can't understand why they're disliked. And so we have a new word:

"secularphobia." In an article titled "Why Americans Hate Atheists: Understanding Secularphobia," Phil Zuckerman, a sociology professor, wrote,

> Last week, the Pew Research Center released the results of a new survey concerning who Americans would want — or rather, wouldn't want — for an in-law. While about 10 percent of Americans said they'd be unhappy if a family member married someone of a different political persuasion . . . nearly 50 percent of Americans said that they'd be unhappy if a family member married an atheist. This finding comes as no surprise. Social science has long revealed high rates of secularphobia — the irrational dislike, distrust, fear, or hatred of nonreligious people — within American society.[89]

He surmises that atheists are disliked by so many Americans because of prejudice — since we equate atheism with "being un-American and/or unpatriotic" — and because believers are basically insecure and nonbelief threatens their "shaky" faith.[90]

The Christian Science Monitor, in an article titled "Ted Cruz: Atheists shouldn't be president. Why are they so vilified?" the writer was mystified about why most Americans are biased against atheists:

> It's a bias that appears to be widespread and largely unchallenged. As *Psychology Today* points out, academic studies have demonstrated that atheist patients are given lower priority on organ donation lists, and atheist parents are more likely to be denied custody rights after a divorce. It is illegal for an atheist to hold

public office in seven states, atheists cannot testify as a witness on trial in Arkansas, they aren't allowed in the Boy Scouts, and Humanist chaplains are barred from serving in the nation's military.[91]

Many wonder how atheists can be prohibited from serving in state offices, when the Constitution bans a religious test. Here is how Article VI reads:

> The Senators and Representatives before mentioned, and the Members of the several State Legislatures, and all executive and judicial Officers, both of the United States and of the several States, shall be bound by Oath or Affirmation, to support this Constitution; but no religious Test shall ever be required as a Qualification to any Office or public Trust under the United States.[92]

Congress cannot require religious tests for an office under the United States government — federal officeholders. The individual states, however, were free at the time of the nation's founding to impose religious tests as they saw fit — and all of them did. State tests limited public offices to Christians or, in some states, only to Protestants. Notice the wording in these state constitutions:

- Maryland (Article 37): "No religious test ought ever to be required as a qualification for any office of profit or trust in this State, other than a declaration of belief in the existence of God. . . ."

- Texas (Article 1, Section 4): "No religious test shall ever be required as a qualification to any office, or public trust, in this State; nor shall any one be excluded from holding office on account of his religious sentiments, provided he acknowledge the existence of a Supreme Being."

- Arkansas (Article 19, Section 1): "No person who denies the being of a God shall hold any office in the civil departments of this State, nor be competent to testify as a witness in any Court."

- Tennessee (Article 9, Section 2): "No person who denies the being of God, or a future state of rewards and punishments, shall hold any office in the civil department of this state."

Why would there be such a requirement? Keep in mind that America is "one nation under God," as declared in our country's Pledge of Allegiance; our national anthem, "The Star-Spangled Banner" (written in 1812) includes the words "In God is our Trust"; and our nation's official motto, "In God We Trust," was first printed on our coins in 1864.

Trust in God is the foundation of our nation. Since America's founding, the tradition has been for oaths to end with "So help me God." Historically, the phrase is included in the oath of office for the president, congressmen and senators, state legislators and employees, jurors, notaries public, and those serving in the military. To become American citizens, immigrants must take the United States Oath of Allegiance, which ends "so help me God." And we have court witnesses swear to "tell the whole truth and nothing but the truth, so help me God."

Our founders understood that people in positions of power would have opportunities to do corrupt deeds for their own benefit. But if they believe in God and in a future state of rewards and punishments, then when tempted to do wrong, they won't give in. Knowing we'll have to give an account to Almighty God helps us to act with honesty and integrity. As George Washington put it in his farewell address: "Let it simply be asked where is the security for property, for reputation, for life, if the sense of religious obligation desert the oaths, which are the instruments of investigation in the Courts of Justice?"

Because atheists have no absolute basis for good and evil, and don't believe in an afterlife, some would say they can't be trusted with public office. Whether this "bias" would stand up to today's Supreme Court scrutiny, it clearly shows the intent of our founders.

Other minority groups have overcome biases, *The Christian Science Monitor* notes, so what would it take for atheists to do so? The author's suggestion: "Charitable acts done in the name of atheism — like Richard Dawkins' Non-Believers Giving Aid campaign, launched after the Haiti earthquake — may help."[93]

Even with a very real fear of terrorism and homegrown violence, the United States still is the freest nation on earth. It is a unique refuge where millions have the liberty to pray and worship God, no matter what their religion. It's therefore a bitter blow that those liberties are being attacked by atheists whose hatred for God outweighs any respect for those ideals or any love and concern for their fellow Americans.

Count how many of their lawsuits are against Muslims, Hindus, Jews, or Buddhists. They are only against Christians. This is because the United States is soaked in a Christian heritage, and that's what is held dear by so many. "In God We Trust" on our money isn't something new. It's been on there for over 150 years.[94]

In truth, these anti-Christian atheists have brought disdain on themselves. They have made themselves odious. They are the playground bully, preying on Christians — those they consider to be weak-minded and meek — knowing that they will turn the other cheek and not pick up a machete.

Prophetic Utterance from Dawkins

For years atheists have been effectively dismantling Christian influence in society, seemingly unaware that another religion — far more restrictive — is attempting to gain power. Consider what Professor Richard Dawkins said about Christianity's decreasing influence:

> There are no Christians, as far as I know, blowing up buildings. I am not aware of any Christian suicide bombers. I am not aware of any major Christian denomination that believes the penalty for apostasy is death. I have mixed feelings about the decline of Christianity, in so far as Christianity might be a bulwark [a defense] against something worse.[95]

Perhaps American atheists don't know what Professor Dawkins knows, because he sees "something worse" happening in his country today. In Britain, Islam is steadily growing and taking control through local governments, with the goal of instituting Sharia law and its harsh punishments. Islam isn't like Christianity. It doesn't love its enemies; it kills them:

> Blasphemy in Islam is any form of cursing, questioning or annoying God, Muhammad or

anything considered sacred in Islam. The sharia of various Islamic schools of jurisprudence specify different punishment for blasphemy against Islam, by Muslims and non-Muslims, ranging from imprisonment, fines, flogging, amputation, hanging, or beheading.[96]

A prominent Nigerian humanist said of the danger of being openly atheist in his home country:

> Expressing atheistic views can easily be interpreted as a form of blasphemy. Blasphemy is a crime punishable by death. Expressing atheistic views can easily be taken to be an insult to Islam or to Allah or to his Prophet Muhammed. . . . So there are two places for an atheist in sharia communities: in the closet or in the grave.[97]

Atheists in America are playing John the Baptist to Islam. By dismantling Christianity's influence in our nation, they are preparing the way and making every path straight.

Chapter Three

A Glimmer of Hope for Political Atheism

There is a glimmer of hope on the horizon about the possibility of one day having an atheist as a viable presidential candidate. It involves a massive group known as "the Millennials." The millennial generation, which consists of those born between 1982 and 2002, is becoming increasingly less religious. In a CNN article, Paul Fidalgo reports:

> While far too many Americans still tell pollsters they could never vote for someone who was gay, lesbian or Muslim, the bottom of this particular political barrel is almost always occupied by atheists. But for all those nonbelievers who keep their hats on their heads rather than toss them into rings, a new Gallup Poll offers a glimmer of hope. . . . The number of those who would refuse to vote for

an atheist candidate has also dropped from where it was in 2012, from 43% to 40%.[98]

While noting it's undeniable that "atheism remains a major obstacle to passing electoral muster," Fidalgo thinks nonbelievers have "moved up a rung." He adds:

> What explains this slow but unmistakable upward trend? A major survey by the Pew Research Center recently revealed that America's religiously unaffiliated, also known as "nones," had for the first time grown to become the second-largest religious identification group in the country, beating out Catholics, and leaping from about 16% in 2007 to 23% just seven years later.[99]

So there lies the atheist's hope: The "nones," a category that includes people who self-identify as atheists or agnostics, as well as those who say their religion is "nothing in particular," now constitute a sizable number of voting-age adults.

That translates to millions of people who overwhelmingly support liberal issues such as homosexual marriage and abortion. But the "nones" aren't as none as they are made out to be. Here's the strange dilemma. Despite their progressive views, *they are favorable toward evangelical candidates.* Cathy Lynn Grossman of Religion News Service writes:

> Millennials are just as likely as members of the Silent Generation to vote for evangelical candidates. That's a bit of a surprise, given what else we know about young voters. There's mounting evidence that they overwhelmingly support marriage equality, anti-discrimination

laws for LGBT people, and reproductive health care access — causes that are anathema to most evangelicals.[100]

Nonetheless, she states, "Atheism isn't about to win anyone any elections, and it's clear that American voters still expect and respond to candidates with professed religious beliefs. . . . Even if an avowed atheist were to enter the race, she'd still be unpopular with most Americans and millennial tolerance wouldn't be enough to propel her to glory."[101] This viewpoint is further confirmed by Gary Scott Smith in *The Washington Post*:

> Given this increase in "nones," especially among younger adults (one-third of all adults younger than 30 are religiously unaffiliated), could an atheist perhaps be elected president? Probably not. In a 2014 Pew Research Center poll, twice as many religiously unaffiliated Americans said they would be less likely to vote for a candidate who does not believe in God (24 percent) as said they would be more likely to do so (12 percent).[102]

A bird can't fly without wings, and no candidate is going to fly into the White House without paying some sort of lip service to God, and it seems the candidates in the 2016 presidential race are aware of this reality. Even if any secretly hold atheist views, they dare not whisper their convictions. Uncomfortable though it may be to profess faith in God, they know it's as much a part of the process as having a good fiscal policy, shaking hands, and kissing babies.

Speaking at a National Religious Liberties Conference in Iowa, presidential hopeful Senator Ted Cruz said he believes (like much of the country) that anyone who wants to be president must fear God and pray daily. He commented, "Any president who doesn't begin every day on his knees isn't fit to be commander-in-chief of this country."[103]

While a popular meme found its way all over the Internet saying that Donald Trump was a closet atheist, it turned out not to be true.[104] However, one could justifiably suspect that he had little or no faith in God. At a Family Leadership Summit, he appeared to be a fish out of water when it came to speaking of his religious faith. According to the *Washington Examiner*, a Republican leader at the event "was dumbfounded by the candidate's views of religion." He stated, "It was Trump's inability to articulate any coherent relationship with God or demonstrate the role faith plays in his life that really sucked the oxygen out of the room."[105]

Hillary Clinton is Methodist by denomination, and it's uncommon to hear her talk about her personal faith in God. However, light can't stay under a bushel if one wants to be president. In the *Washington Post*, Daniel Silliman writes, "Voters consistently say they want politicians to have faith, yet they often don't believe them when they talk about it. For Clinton, this seems especially true." He reports:

> Speaking from a Methodist pulpit on Sunday morning, Hillary Clinton explained her political vision with a reference to the classic Sunday school song "This Little Light of Mine." "Too many people," she said, "want to let their light shine, but they can't get out from under that bushel basket. It is way too heavy to lift alone. And that's where the village comes in."[106]

Not everyone believes that she (or even President Obama) has any light:

> HBO talk show host Bill Maher said in a Monday interview with the "Daily Show's" Jon Stewart that he does not find President Barack Obama's Christian faith to be genuine, arguing that he is really an atheist, and mocked former U.S. Secretary of State Hillary Clinton's recent comments that the Bible is her biggest influence.[107]

Whether the candidates' statements about God are sincerely held beliefs or political posturing, they'd better keep it to themselves if they want a hope of capturing the White House.

Are Atheists Hopeful?

Jesse Ventura, the outspoken former wrestler and one-term Independent governor of Minnesota, irked the organizers of a nationwide prayer event when he declined to proclaim a National Day of Prayer in his state — the only 1 of 50 governors not to issue the declaration. He later "came out of the closet," as he put it, adding that he's "proud" to be called an atheist.

While he has toyed with running for public office again, when he appeared on *The Howard Stern Show* in 2011, Ventura said that he wasn't hopeful:

> I don't believe you can be an atheist and admit it and get elected in our country.[108]

Staunch atheist Penn Jillette, of the magic/comedy duo Penn & Teller, gave his thoughts on whether an atheist would ever occupy the Oval Office:

Some of my fellow atheists bemoan that atheism is the final taboo in politics — polls report that America would never elect an atheist president. Because of that, they brag that their favorite candidate (usually Obama or a Clinton) has to lie and say they believe in god and promise that they pray for supernatural guidance in world affairs. . . . The Clintons and Obamas swear they believe that their lives and our country are guided by a supreme-being. I take them at their word. If the choice is superstitious straight-shooter or a patronizing liar, I'll go with honest. At least the supernatural has some rules.[109]

Notice that even though he is condescending toward those he calls "superstitious," Jillette knows that people who believe in the God revealed in the Bible are governed by a higher ethic. Knowing they will be held accountable for their actions, they are more trustworthy and reliable. (This is why, when it comes to a role where trust is essential, like a daycare worker, people prefer a God-fearing employee over an atheist.) Jillette added,

I'm not president, but I do a magic show. Teller and I are atheists and our audiences are mostly believers and they don't care what we don't believe because we're the ones they want to see do a magic show. If Americans can take honesty in their magicians, we should give them a chance to accept honesty in their president.[110]

As much as I appreciate the skill of a magician to fool his audience, it's a massive leap to compare the deception of sleight-of-hand to the presidency of the United States. This office carries the responsibility of commanding our military, and as Commander-in-Chief, his decisions can mean life or death for all those who serve our country. His selection of judges — to district and appellate courts as well as the Supreme Court, with lifelong appointments — can impact the course of the nation for generations to come. His choices can determine life or death for the unborn, redefine the institution of marriage and the meaning of family, shape the economy, and affect our personal freedoms. His belief in (or denial of) God will determine his decisions and the direction of the entire nation. Either Mr. Jillette thinks too highly of his own profession or he thinks too little of the office of the president.

Jillette concludes:

> Maybe Americans are too stupid and big-oted to elect the right person for the job even if he or she is an atheist, but we haven't run that experiment yet and until we do, I will not take atheists' condescending guesses on faith. I don't have faith — I'm an atheist.[111]

It seems that average Americans aren't as stupid as some would suggest. They esteem the office of the president and understand their responsibility to vote for someone who has genuine honesty and integrity. They don't want to experiment with an atheist in the White House when human lives, morality, and the country's economy are in the balance.

If you're an atheist who believes (in faith) that an honest-to-God atheist would be a good candidate for the presidency, don't hold your breath. There is currently little hope for the American people to elect an atheist president in our lifetime — or beyond.

So how is it that, according to atheists, some in their ranks have already made it to the presidency? We will look at this in the next chapter.

Chapter Four

How Many Presidents Have Been Atheists?

Atheists maintain that, to date, the United States has actually had four presidents who were atheists. They cite Thomas Jefferson, Abraham Lincoln, George Washington, and James Madison.

All four are listed on websites such as Positive Atheism and Celebrity Atheist with a collection of quotations designed to make them appear atheistic. However, both of these atheist sites are having trouble with the truth. Let's look at each of these men and consider their own words about God.

Thomas Jefferson

In an article exploring whether an atheist could ever be president, *The Washington Post* gets to the truth of the matter about Jefferson, "the only candidate in American history charged with being an atheist":

Federalists repeatedly attacked him as an infidel who would destroy the nation's Christian foundations and staunchly promote secularism. Several factors kept Jefferson from being defeated. Most important, the accusations were false — he believed in God, repeatedly affirmed God's providence, and frequently worshiped in Episcopal churches, so many discounted these attacks as mere political partisanship.[112]

Jefferson, selected to write the original draft of the Declaration of Independence, is credited with being its author. In it, he cites four references to God. After acknowledging God as the Lawgiver ("the Laws of Nature and of Nature's God"), Jefferson then identifies Him as our Creator, Judge, and Protector:

We hold these truths to be self-evident, that all men are created equal, that they are endowed by *their Creator* with certain unalienable Rights, that among these are Life, Liberty and the pursuit of Happiness. . . .

We, therefore . . . appealing to the *Supreme Judge of the world* for the rectitude of our intentions . . . declare, that these United Colonies are, and of Right ought to be Free and Independent States. . . .

And for the support of this Declaration, with a firm reliance on the protection of divine Providence, we mutually pledge to each other our Lives, our Fortunes and our sacred Honor.[113]

Jefferson later reiterated similar ideas, that God gave us life and will one day be our Judge:

God who gave us life gave us liberty. And can the liberties of a nation be thought secure when we have removed their only firm basis, a conviction in the minds of the people that these liberties are of the gift of God? That they are not to be violated but with his wrath? Indeed I tremble for my country when I reflect that God is just: that his justice cannot sleep forever.[114]

In a letter to Benjamin Rush, Jefferson clearly stated that he was no atheist:

To the corruptions of Christianity I am indeed, opposed; but not to the genuine precepts of Jesus himself. I am a Christian, in the only sense in which he wished any one to be; sincerely attached to his doctrines, in preference to all others.[115]

Abraham Lincoln

Not only was Lincoln not an atheist, but he wouldn't vote for one, either. After his political opponent spread rumors that Lincoln was a religious scoffer, Lincoln wrote in a public statement refuting the charges: "I do not think I could myself, be brought to support a man for office, whom I knew to be an open enemy of, and scoffer at, religion."[116]

As for his beliefs, Honest Abe was honest only because he feared God. He believed that he was ultimately responsible to his Creator. He told Congress that each of us will be held accountable in eternity:

In times like the present, men should utter nothing for which they would not willingly be responsible through time and eternity.[117]

Abraham Lincoln also directed his thanks to God for his personal political victories:

> I am thankful to God for this approval of the people ... I give thanks to the Almighty for this evidence of the people's resolution to stand by free government and the rights of humanity.[118]

Here Lincoln speaks of his love of the Bible and his thankfulness to God for giving it to humanity:

> In regard to this Great Book, I have but to say, it is the best gift God has given to man. All the good the Savior gave to the world was communicated through this book. But for it we could not know right from wrong. All things most desirable for man's welfare, here and hereafter, are to be found portrayed in it.[119]

One who recognizes the Bible as a gift from God and the source of morality, believes in eternal life, and acknowledges the Savior — as Lincoln does here — is not an atheist. Following are Lincoln's thoughts about his prayer-life and his dependence on God:

> I have been driven many times upon my knees by the overwhelming conviction that I had nowhere else to go. My own wisdom, and that of all about me, seemed insufficient for the day.[120]

President Barack Obama quoted these words of Lincoln before inviting the American people to likewise call out to God:

NOW, THEREFORE, I, BARACK OBAMA, President of the United States of America, do hereby proclaim May 5, 2011, as a National Day of Prayer. I invite all citizens of our Nation, as their own faith or conscience directs them, to join me in giving thanks for the many blessings we enjoy, and I ask all people of faith to join me in asking God for guidance, mercy, and protection for our Nation.[121]

George Washington

Here are just a few of the many thoughts of our first president, "the father of his country," in reference to God and prayer:

> I now make it my earnest prayer that God would . . . most graciously be pleased to dispose us all to do justice, to love mercy, and to demean ourselves with that charity, humility, and pacific temper of the mind which were the characteristics of the Divine Author of our blessed religion.[122]

> You do well to wish to learn our arts and ways of life, and above all, the religion of Jesus Christ. These will make you a greater and happier people than you are.[123]

> While we are zealously performing the duties of good citizens and soldiers, we certainly ought not to be inattentive to the higher duties of religion. To the distinguished character of Patriot, it should be our highest glory to add the more distinguished character of Christian.[124]

In his memorable Farewell Address, our beloved first president reiterated the importance of religion in the life of our nation — not only in the citizens but in all who take the oaths of office:

> Of all the dispositions and habits which lead to political prosperity, Religion and Morality are indispensable supports. In vain would that man claim the tribute of Patriotism, who should labor to subvert these great pillars of human happiness, these firmest props of the duties of Men and Citizens. . . . Let it simply be asked where is the security for property, for reputation, for life, if the sense of religious obligation desert the oaths, which are the instruments of investigation in Courts of Justice? And let us with caution indulge the supposition, that morality can be maintained without religion. Whatever may be conceded to the influence of refined education on minds of peculiar structure; reason and experience both forbid us to expect that national morality can prevail in exclusion of religious principle.[125]

James Madison

James Madison, the Chief Architect of the Constitution, was, like the others we've looked at, a believer in God and not an atheist. He said,

> A watchful eye must be kept on ourselves lest, while we are building ideal monuments of renown and bliss here, we neglect to have our names enrolled in the Annals of Heaven.[126]

The belief in a God All Powerful wise and good, is so essential to the moral order of the World and to the happiness of man, that arguments which enforce it cannot be drawn from too many sources.[127]

I have sometimes thought there could not be a stronger testimony in favor of religion or against temporal enjoyments, even the most rational and manly, than for men who occupy the most honorable and gainful departments and are rising in reputation and wealth, publicly to declare their unsatisfactoriness by becoming fervent advocates in the cause of Christ; and I wish you may give in your evidence in this way.[128]

Benjamin Franklin

Though he was never president, Benjamin Franklin served our country in many other roles, and is another Founding Father who is said to be an atheist. Steven Shaw, who compiled a list of "clearly confirmed atheists" for AskMen.com, said, "One of the most famous men in American history, and regarded as the most intelligent of those who signed the Declaration of Independence, Franklin is a surprise addition to this list."[129] Let's see if he belongs on their list:

Forasmuch as ingratitude is one of the most odious of vices, let me not be unmindful gratefully to acknowledge the favors I receive from Heaven. . . . For all Thy innumerable benefits; for life, and reason, and the use of speech; for health; and joy; and every pleasant hour — my Good God, I thank Thee.[130]

I have lived, Sir, a long time, and the longer I live, the more convincing proofs I see of this truth — *that God governs in the affairs of men.* And if a sparrow cannot fall to the ground without his notice, is it probable that an empire can rise without his aid? We have been assured, Sir, in the Sacred Writings, that "except the Lord build the House, they labour in vain that build it." I firmly believe this; and I also believe that without his concurring aid, we shall succeed in this political building no better than the builders of Babel.[131]

In a letter to Ezra Stiles (president of Yale College), written just a month before he died, Franklin cited his beliefs in great detail:

Here is my Creed: I believe in one God, Creator of the Universe. That he governs it by his Providence. That he ought to be worshipped. That the most acceptable Service we can render to him, is doing Good to his other Children. That the Soul of Man is immortal, and will be treated with Justice in another Life respecting its Conduct in this. . . . As to Jesus of Nazareth, my opinion of whom you particularly desire, I think the system of morals and his religion as he left them to us, the best the world ever saw, or is likely to see.[132]

As the atheist website *Free Thought* rightfully conceded, "None of the Founding Fathers were atheists."[133] Still, these four men are firmly carved in stone on atheist websites as firmly as the four who are depicted on Mount Rushmore, apparently in an effort to bolster the faith of the faithless.

Chapter Five

The Atheist's Character

I am friends with a number of atheists. I have had meals with many, including David Silverman, the president of American Atheists, Inc., who is very likeable and friendly. Others have great senses of humor, and we are able to enjoy each other's company despite our differing worldviews. Having said that, I have to say the hatred that many atheists have for Christianity is *very* real. In part, this is because the idea of a God to whom we are accountable threatens every sinful sexual pleasure for which most atheist males live. (Is it any wonder that over two-thirds of atheists are men?[134])

Atheism gives them license to feast on porn, indulge in fornication, engage in homosexuality, and commit adultery without any sense of guilt. It means that they can lie to meet an end, love money, blaspheme God's holy name, and steal if they think they can justify it. They believe there's no absolute right or wrong, so if something makes them happy, then it's fair game. That includes suing the shirt off those they are convinced want to throw the huge wet blanket of Christianity over their pleasures. It also includes vilifying Christians, in an attempt to discredit the message of Christianity.

Atheists have spread disgusting lies about me, writing sickening words and putting my name and picture with them: "If The Lord commanded me to rape and kill my own children tonight it would be done by morning."[135] (This was written by a middle-aged atheist in Chicago.) Then they post questions online like: "Christians would you rape and kill your own children if God told you to like Ray Comfort?"[136] Atheists have called me racist, and falsely claimed that I believe cancer is a gift from God and that people with cancer shouldn't visit doctors.[137]

So I regularly have angry atheists demanding I be locked up, and some even saying they would like to kill me. For an atheist, apparently the vigilante taking of a human life can be justified.

When I wrote a book titled *You Can Lead an Atheist to Evidence, But You Can't Make Him Think* and it bumped Richard Dawkins's book off the number one spot in Amazon's "Atheist" category, we discovered that over two hundred atheists decided to give it a bad review to bring down its rating. They did the same thing with our movie on the subject of homosexuality, called *Audacity*.[138] Out of a 1–10 rating, over 1,500 of them gave it a 1 rating on IMDb.com.[139] Atheists have had the police visit my home to investigate repulsive and bogus claims, and have done numerous other things to try to malign my character — all because they hate God and those who believe in Him. This comes with the territory for Christians, as Jesus informed His followers:

Blessed are you when they revile and per-
secute you, and say all kinds of evil against
you falsely for My sake. Rejoice and be exceed-
ingly glad, for great is your reward in heaven,
for so they persecuted the prophets who were
before you (Matthew 5:11–12).

Some atheists hate Christians for the same reason criminals hate the police. Some criminals will even kill an
officer of the law, not because of who he is, but because
of what he represents. The policeman stands for what
is right, while the criminal loves to do what is wrong.
Atheists, like criminals, are similar to creatures of the
night that scatter when light shines:

And this is the condemnation, that the
light has come into the world, and men loved
darkness rather than light, because their deeds
were evil. For everyone practicing evil hates
the light and does not come to the light, lest
his deeds should be exposed (John 3:19–20).

Even a Nativity Scene Offends Them

Atheists despise the light of Christ and do everything
they can to extinguish it —including the commemo-
ration of His birth. Christmas is almost unanimously
celebrated in America, and atheists seem to forget that
its observance has been a federally recognized holiday
since 1870. Yet that doesn't keep many from fighting
against any official depiction of it.

Atheists in Lincoln, Nebraska, highjacked the local
nativity scene and replaced it with their own display,
in the name of "tolerance":

When Christmas comes to Lincoln, Nebraska this year, Mary, Joseph and the baby

Jesus will find there is no room in the inner halls of the state capitol — and no manger either. Instead, there will be an 8ft "happy humanist" next to a "reason tree" dedicated to science and "human intellectual achievement." In Lincoln, amid the supposed "war on Christmas" bemoaned each year by the political right, it appears the atheists really have stolen Christmas.[140]

In December 2015, *Time* magazine reported that atheists displayed a mock nativity scene at the Texas State Capitol. Placed there by the Freedom From Religion Foundation, it consisted of Benjamin Franklin, the Statue of Liberty, Thomas Jefferson, and George Washington gathered around a manger containing the Bill of Rights. The governor complained that the display "deliberately mocks Christians and Christianity":

> The Biblical scene of the newly born Jesus Christ lying in a manger in Bethlehem lies at the very heart of the Christian faith. Subjecting an image held sacred by millions of Texans to the Foundation's tasteless sarcasm does nothing to promote morals and the general welfare.[141]

This mocking and ridicule of God is not unusual for nonbelievers. Look at the Bible's description of the character of an atheist:

> And even as they did not like to retain God in their knowledge, God gave them over to a debased mind, to do those things which are not fitting; being filled with all unrighteousness,

sexual immorality, wickedness, covetousness, maliciousness; full of envy, murder, strife, deceit, evil-mindedness; they are whisperers, backbiters, haters of God, violent, proud, boasters, inventors of evil things, disobedient to parents, undiscerning, untrustworthy, unloving, unforgiving, unmerciful; who, knowing the righteous judgment of God, that those who practice such things are deserving of death, not only do the same but also approve of those who practice them (Romans 1:28–32).

This is an accurate description of modern aggressive atheists. They are proud, untrustworthy "haters of God." This has become evident to many because of the incessant lawsuits attempting to remove any mention of God. These are not the typical character traits most voters look for in their elected officials, so is it any wonder that for atheists the most powerful position in the world remains out of reach?

Our country has enough politicians who will say one thing to get elected only to do whatever they please once in office. They regularly prove the truth of the saying "Power tends to corrupt," as we read scandal after scandal of elected officials who are more concerned with meeting their own selfish desires than being a selfless public servant. And this usually comes from the same people who claim to believe in a Supreme Being who will one day hold them accountable!

To give the most powerful position in the world to someone who doesn't even have a moral rudder —but who alone determines right and wrong for himself — would be the height of foolishness and lead to devastating consequences for our great nation.

So nowadays, if someone is an out-of-the-closet atheist who wants to run for political office, he may as well change his name to Judas Benedict Arnold.

Chapter Six

Sweden, the Atheist Nation

F or years atheists have maintained that Christianity is on the way out (thanks in part to their efforts) and that atheism is on the way in, especially in countries such as Sweden. It is said that in Sweden and Denmark, where "non-belief or even outright atheism is widespread, atheists can go about their lives free from the fear that their lack of belief will cause people to mistrust, hate, or even discriminate against them."[142] Notable atheist Sam Harris argues that Scandinavian countries, which are much more secular than the United States, have much lower rates of many social ills, including crime, drug use, teen pregnancy, and poverty,[143] and Sweden is touted by atheists as among the happiest countries in the world due to its lack of religion.[144]

So is Sweden really a predominantly atheist nation? Phil Zuckerman, author of *Society without God* and an outspoken atheist, reported that several academic surveys have, in recent years, found the number of Swedes who say they do not believe in God varied from 46 percent to 85 percent, yet another survey reported that only 17 percent of respondents self-identified as "atheist."[145]

A 2015 poll by WIN/Gallup International stated, "The Swedish prove to be the least religious in the Western World with 78% saying they are either not religious or convinced atheists."[146] Yet in 2012, only 8 percent of Swedes were reported to be atheist.[147] So what accounts for the great disparity in findings? What do Swedes really believe?

One clue is that almost 9 out of 10 Swedes have Christian burials,[148] and the last thing a die-hard atheist would request is a Christian burial. In a *New York Times* article, tellingly called "Scandinavian Nonbelievers, Which Is Not to Say Atheists," the author noted:

> Mr. Zuckerman, a sociologist who teaches at Pitzer College in Claremont, Calif., has reported his findings on religion in Denmark and Sweden in "Society Without God" (New York: University Press, 2008). Much that he found will surprise many people, as it did him. The many nonbelievers he interviewed, both informally and in structured, taped and transcribed sessions, *were anything but antireligious*, for example. They typically *balked at the label "atheist."* An overwhelming majority had in fact been baptized, and many had been confirmed or married in church.[149]

So the many Swedish nonbelievers he interviewed were anything but antireligious and typically balked at the label "atheist." The article also notes that *"they called themselves Christians*, and most were content to remain in the Danish National Church or the Church of Sweden, the traditional national branches of Lutheranism."[150]

This is perhaps the reason there's such confusion with the numbers:

> There is a difference between people who consider themselves atheists and non-religious people. *Non-religious people simply don't follow any rules or guides of a religion, but they may believe in God.* Atheists have a lack of belief in religion and God altogether.[151]

So for those who consider the Nordic country to be an atheist paradise, and hope to create the same environment in the United States, they'll have to look elsewhere for inspiration.

Famous Atheist Leaders

Well-known atheist political leaders may be hard to find, but they do exist. Every Communist leader, for example, has publicly declared his atheism. Throughout history, there have been 28 countries whose regimes have been ruled by avowed atheists. According to one count, these regimes have been led by 89 atheists, more than half of whom have engaged in murderous acts similar to those of Stalin and Mao.

Let's look at what a few of these notable nonbelievers have achieved:

- Benito Mussolini: Italian fascist dictator, friend and ally of Adolf Hitler, was responsible for 430,000 deaths.[152] After he was executed by his own people, his face was beaten until it was disfigured and his body was hung upside down on meat hooks.[153]

- Karl Marx: His ideas lead to the deaths of more than 90 million people — murdered, starved to death, or shot as "traitors."[154]

- Joseph Stalin: Most estimates of deaths attributed to his regime from reputed scholars and historians range between 20 and 60 million. "If the figure of 60 million dead is accurate that would mean that an average of 2 million were killed during each year of Stalin's horrific reign — or 40,000 every week."[155]

- Mao Zedong: His policies and political purges caused the deaths of 49 to 78 million people.[156]

- Vladimir Lenin: Between 50,000 and 200,000 were executed as "enemies of the state," tens of thousands died in prison, and 5 million starved to death.[157]

Dr. R.J. Rummel, professor emeritus of political science at the University of Hawaii, estimates that since 1900, the total body count is approximately 262 million dead at the bloody hands of atheistic governments. Rummel, who first coined the term "democide" (death by government), wrote:

> Just to give perspective on this incredible murder by government, if all these bodies were laid head to toe, with the average height being 5', then they would circle the earth ten times. Also, this democide murdered 6 times more people than died in combat in all the foreign and internal wars of the century.[158]

With a "58 percent chance that an atheist leader will murder a noticeable percentage of the population over which he rules,"[159] the common atheist assertion that a godless society will be a peaceful one just isn't historically accurate.

Atheists also frequently claim that it is religion that is the source of most of the wars in the world. However, *The Encyclopedia of Wars*[160] says that, as of 2004, there have been 1,763 wars during human history, 123 of which could be called religious in nature. That means that religious wars constitute fewer than 7 percent of all wars, and over half were in the name of Islam. Most of the rest — 93 percent of all wars — were political in nature.

The World's Largest Atheist Nation

Rarely do nonbelievers boast that communist China has the world's largest atheist population.[161] But consider what is happening in China. An article in *The Economist* called "Cracks in the Atheist Edifice" tells of a revival of Christianity taking place in the world's biggest atheist nation. *The Economist* is a secular, non-Conservative publication that espouses "cultural liberalism" and legal recognition for same-sex marriage. It has no axe to grind on this issue:

> Christianity is hard to control in China, and getting harder all the time. It is spreading rapidly, and infiltrating the party's own ranks. The line is blurring between house churches and official ones, and Christians are starting to emerge from hiding to play a more active part in society. The Communist Party has to find a new way to deal with all this. There is even talk that the party, the world's

largest explicitly atheist organization, might follow its sister parties in Vietnam and Cuba and allow members to embrace a dogma other than — even higher than — that of Marx.[162]

This isn't a mere drop in the bucket. There is a tsunami of Christianity flooding atheist China:

> There were perhaps three million Catholics and one million Protestants when the party came to power in 1949. Officials now say there are between 23 million and 40 million, all told. In 2010 the Pew Research Centre, an American polling organization, estimated there were 58 million Protestants and 9 million Catholics. Many experts, foreign and Chinese, now accept that there are probably more Christians than there are members of the 87 million-strong Communist Party. Most are evangelical Protestants.[163]

God is at work among the millions in China and other countries. Those who are not familiar with biblical Christianity don't know that the flame they're trying to extinguish is like a fire among stubble. The harder the winds of persecution blow, the greater the fire takes hold.

In the next chapter we will look at something atheists have in common with religious people.

Chapter Seven

The Atheist's Big Mistake

Atheists might be surprised to learn they have something in common with almost every religious person. When it comes to the most important issue in life — how we can find everlasting life — almost all atheists (as do religious people) think that an individual's salvation is dependent on being a good person. They think Christians strive to be good — to not steal, lie, or commit adultery; to love their neighbor; etc. — in an effort to earn their right to heaven.

Atheists therefore often strive to be seen as "just as morally good" as those who believe in God. *USA Today* published an article called "As atheists know, you can be good without God,"[164] and "Good without God" is one of atheists' favorite catch-phrases for banners and billboards.[165]

For example, consider what atheist Patrick Horst advised the religiously unaffiliated gathered at a "Nashville Nones Convention":

> Shock them [theists] not only with the fact
> that you as a secular person know what you
> believe and why, but the way you live it makes
> you a kind and compassionate and often times
> even a better person than they might be.[166]

In "Good Without God — But Better Without God?"
secular humanist Ronald Lindsay writes, "The traditional knock on nonbelievers, including humanists, has
always been that one can't be 'good without God.' "
Again, this misconception is the same error made by
every religious person who is striving to earn God's
favor through their religious good works. Christians,
on the other hand, know that no one is good in God's
eyes. The dictionary has more than 40 definitions of
the word "good"; the number one definition is "moral
excellence." That's the standard with which God will
judge humanity. The Bible says that almost every man
will proclaim his own goodness, and that we are all
pure in our *own* eyes (see Proverbs 20:6, 16:2). We will
continue to think that we are morally good (because
we have our *own* definition of good) until we compare
ourselves to God's perfect standard.

So let's look for a moment at the Ten Commandments, God's moral Law, to see if we qualify as morally "good."

How many lies do you think you've told in your
whole life, including "little white lies"? Have you ever
taken anything that didn't belong to you, irrespective of
its value? Almost everyone I have ever spoken with has
lied or stolen at least once. Have you? We tend to forget unpleasant thoughts, or memories that make us feel
guilty, but God doesn't. He remembers your thoughts
as though they just happened. So be ruthlessly honest
with yourself, because if you don't admit your sins now,
on Judgment Day it will be too late to ask for mercy.

Have you ever used God's name in vain (without due respect), saying "Jesus" or "OMG" as "just a meaningless expression"? God's name is holy, and to use it as a cuss word is a terrible sin called blasphemy.

Jesus said, "Whoever looks at a woman to lust for her has already committed adultery with her in his heart." Have you ever looked with lust? This is the Bible verse that showed me that I was in big trouble on Judgment Day. I didn't realize that God saw my thought-life. It was as though a light went on in my darkened mind. If God made my eyes, He's not blind. If He made my ears, He's not deaf. If He created my brain, He can see what He created. It was a revelation that brought very sobering implications.

If you have done these things, God sees you as a lying, thieving, blasphemous adulterer at heart. Do you still think that you are good? Is a lying thief a good person? Are you morally excellent? Of course you're not. Like me, and everyone else, you are a sinner. Look at Psalm 14:

> The fool has said in his heart, "There is no God." They are corrupt, they have done abominable works, there is none who does good. The LORD looks down from heaven upon the children of men, to see if there are any who understand, who seek God. They have all turned aside, they have together become corrupt; there is none who does good, no, not one. (Psalm 14:1–3).

When we compare ourselves to God's standard of goodness, we can see that, in truth, you and I are heading for hell. But the Bible says that God is rich in mercy toward those who fear Him. As sinners, we broke God's moral Law and deserve to be punished, and God's place of punishment is a prison called hell. But Jesus paid our fine for us by dying on the Cross for our sins. If you stand guilty in court, and someone steps forward and pays your fine, the judge can legally let you go, even though you are guilty. God can dismiss our case and let us live forever because of what Jesus did on the Cross: "For God so loved the world that He gave His only begotten Son, that whoever believes in Him should not perish but have everlasting life" (John 3:16). Three days later, Jesus rose from the dead, defeating death.

Salvation isn't something any of us could ever earn by being "good." Instead, it is a free gift of God if you will repent (turn from your sin) and trust in Jesus alone (as you'd trust a parachute). When you jump out of a plane with a parachute firmly strapped around you, you don't flap your arms thinking you could add anything to the effort. Your parachute is all you need to land safely, and you can trust it completely. Today, stop trusting in your goodness (you don't have any) and trust completely in Jesus and His finished work on the Cross. Do it now. Apologize to God, and willfully entrust yourself into the hands of Jesus for your eternal salvation.

Again, get right with God today; you may not have tomorrow. Over 54 million people die every year (that's 150,000 every day!). Then read the Bible daily and obey it.[167]

In the end, our "goodness" (doing good things) has nothing to do with earning our way into heaven. Eternal life comes by God's mercy — something that can never be earned. Look at Isaiah 64:6:

> But we are all like an unclean thing, and all our righteousnesses are like filthy rags; we all fade as a leaf, and our iniquities, like the wind, have taken us away.

God's Word says *all* of our righteousnesses (our "good" works) are like "filthy rags" to a holy God! Any goodness we exhibit as Christians comes out of gratitude to God for His kindness, not as an attempt to bribe Him to forgive our sins.

Newton and Atheism

Another fundamental mistake atheists make — the most crucial one — involves their view of God. Sir Isaac Newton said, "Opposition to godliness is atheism in profession and idolatry in practice. Atheism is so senseless and odious to mankind that it never had many professors."

Notice how he linked atheism to idolatry. He said "atheism in profession *and idolatry in practice.*" Few nowadays even know that an "idolater" is someone who has a wrong image of the Creator; he has to make up his own god in his mind.

Arguably the greatest sin of America today was also the greatest sin of Israel in Old Testament times. It is so prevalent that God saw fit to address it in the first two of the Ten Commandments (see Exodus 20). This is because it opens the door to many evils. Israel continually lost her fear of God, strayed into idolatry, and opened a massive can of sinful worms.

The sin of idolatry is often used to justify lying, stealing — even murdering the innocent in His name, like an abortionist who said, "I am proud of what I do. . . . I will continue to follow my conscience and God-given calling of being an abortion care provider."[168]

Joaquin Guzman, the infamous Mexican drug lord known as "El Chapo," proudly claimed, "I supply more heroin, methamphetamine, cocaine and marijuana than anybody else in the world. I have a fleet of submarines, airplanes, trucks and boats."[169] In January 2016, six months after escaping Mexico's most secure prison, he said, "All I did was ask God, and things worked out. Everything was perfect. I'm here, thank God."[170]

The average atheist bases his atheism on his imagination — his own image of what the Creator would be like, if He existed. And he usually sees God as being homophobic, hateful, judgmental, and vindictive. Richard Dawkins adds a few choice words to the image:

> The God of the Old Testament is arguably the most unpleasant character in all fiction: jealous and proud of it; a petty, unjust, unforgiving control-freak; a vindictive, bloodthirsty ethnic cleanser; a misogynistic, homophobic, racist, infanticidal, genocidal, filicidal, pestilential, megalomaniacal, sadomasochistic, capriciously malevolent bully.[171]

Professor Dawkins created what is called "a straw man," a false image he can easily reject, rather than believing the Scriptures which speak of God's true nature — His revelation of Himself. The Bible does show that God is fearfully just, absolutely holy, very angry at sin, justly vengeful toward evil, but that He is also kind, loving, and rich in mercy. All these divine attributes were displayed at the Cross.

Turning Off the Light

When I'm speaking with an atheist about the things of God, I am aware that the Bible says I'm speaking with a "fool" (see Psalm 14:1). This isn't someone who is a clown. Neither is it necessarily someone who has a low IQ. Rather, it's someone who has willfully turned off the inner light that God has given to every man. Each of us has a God-given intuition that we have a Creator, but some choose not to retain God in their knowledge (see Romans 1). Jesus addressed such a person when He said,

> But if your eye is bad, your whole body will be full of darkness. If therefore the light that is in you is darkness, how great is that darkness! (Matthew 6:23).

Turning off that light is a fearful state in which to be, because it leads to a "reprobate mind," where God gives us over to darkness. This is what we often see in contemporary society. Women are viciously raped and murdered, and the perpetrators have no remorse. Teenagers kill their parents; gunmen shoot down schoolchildren, showing themselves to be truly evil, yet there is no contrition. It's as though they are beasts with no conscience. There is "no fear of God before their eyes" (Romans 3:18).

An atheist's philosophy therefore automatically disqualifies him from "reasonable" conversation about God, and if he closes his mind to reason, the conversation will go nowhere. Again, he does this because atheism gives him the temporary license to live his own life the way he chooses, and commit guiltless sexual (and other) sins without a sense of moral responsibility to a Creator. There's a reason that when Jesus listed the evil in the heart of men, sexual sins were at the top of the list (see Mark 7:21). Galatians 5:19 also lists them first: "Now the works of the flesh are evident, which are: adultery, fornication, uncleanness, lewdness. . . ."

Atheism removes any sense of guilt. For a sin-loving sinner it's a delirious dream come true, so he will say anything to defend those pleasures, including deny that which is as obvious as the nose on his face:

the existence of God. We all have enough light to see that He exists:

> For the wrath of God is revealed from heaven against all ungodliness and unrighteousness of men, who suppress the truth in unrighteousness, because what may be known of God is manifest in them, for God has shown it to them. For since the creation of the world His invisible attributes are clearly seen, being understood by the things that are made, even His eternal power and Godhead, so that they are without excuse (Romans 1:18–20).

We are without excuse. We intuitively know that the Creator exists.

Irrefutable Evidence

Late in 2015, I went to a local college to film interviews with atheist students, and I took along a book called *Made in Heaven*, which I co-wrote with an aerospace engineer. It showcases well-known inventions that were copied from nature — such as the "cat's eye" reflectors that illuminate our roads at night (inspired by cat eyes). Engineers and inventors have looked to fish, squids, and shrimp to design such high-tech inventions as body armor, jet propulsion, and optical media. They also copied mosquitoes for the syringe, kingfishers for the nose of high-speed jets, etc. There are over 30 examples in the publication, all displayed in living color.

But I didn't merely show those who professed atheism the cover of the book. I put it into their hands, and let them feel it and examine its color photos and wording. I told them to look through it for a moment, taking special note of the beauty and complexity of the images.

Then I asked them if they could believe that wood pulp came from nowhere and was compressed into smooth, white pages, then ink fell from nowhere and formed itself into those stunning color photos. Could they believe that — all through mindless chance — black ink then fell onto the pages as readable letters and punctuation, forming coherent sentences; that page numbers appeared on the evolved pages, in perfect numerical order; and that the book bound itself and designed its own cover? Then I asked, "Do you believe a book could happen by accident?" Almost all of them said that it was impossible.

I then asked them to define DNA. Deoxyribonucleic acid, as most know nowadays, is what scientists call "the instruction book for life." It is the genetic information encoded within the cell of every living thing that instructs each cell in our body how to grow and how to function. It's our genes that determine whether our skin will be dark or light, our eyes brown or blue, our hair brunette or blond, our height tall or not-so-tall, and so on. Whether we're humans, fish, animals, insects, or plant life, the way our bodies look and operate has all been pre-written in the amazing book of our DNA.

To liken DNA to a book is a gross understatement. The amount of information in the three billion base pairs in the DNA in every human cell is equivalent to that in a thousand books of encyclopedia size.[172] If the DNA instructions in your body's 100 trillion cells were put end-to-end, they would reach to the sun and back over six hundred times; they are so complex and so comprehensive.

Aside from the immense volume of information that your DNA contains, consider whether all the intricate, interrelated parts of this "book" could have come together by sheer chance. Physical chemist Charles Thaxton explains that DNA consists of four bases (adenine, thymine, guanine, and cytosine) that "serve as the 'letters' of a genetic alphabet. They combine in various sequences to form words, sentences, and paragraphs."[173]

This "how-to book" can be "read" under a microscope, and its letters and words are organized into what scientists call "chapters":

> Just as in a book, these letters are grouped in a specific order to communicate a particular idea or task. These orders are written in the language that messenger ribonucleic acid (mRNA) can understand. . . . The mRNA knows where to bind to DNA to make the gene's RNA copy by "reading" the DNA for the start point sequence, or "word," that is coded by the nitrogen bases. . . . The instructions for synthesizing different proteins are organized in the DNA strand into "chapters" called genes.[174]

Like a book, DNA's chapters are even ordered into book sections and are bound together:

> Just like an instructional or "how-to" book found at your local library, the information held within a DNA molecule is organized into sections and can be broken down to letters that code for different commands depending upon their sequence. Keeping with the library book metaphor, DNA is also stored neatly into chromosomes with molecules similar to a book's bindings.[175]

Then I would ask the students I was interviewing this question: "How would you describe the mentality of someone who believed that a physical book would happen by accident?" Their answers were often shaped by political correctness, but ranged from "slow mentally" to "crazy!" This is because it didn't take a rocket scientist to know that such a scenario is completely outside the realm of possibility. No physical book has ever made itself.

Then I asked the students this one simple, seven-word, scientific question: "Do you believe DNA happened by accident?" (These interviews of a number of university students were made into a fascinating one-hour movie. You can watch the result freely at TheAtheistDelusion.com.) If the professed atheist was reasonable, he or she would immediately concede that such a thought was absurd. If one book making itself from nothing is completely outside the realm of possibility, then the instruction book for life making itself is utterly impossible! To even consider it for a moment would be irrational craziness.

DNA's complexity (for any sin-loving sinner who is honest) instantly shows the absurdity of atheism, which holds that the unspeakably amazing instruction book for life happened by chance. It made itself . . . from nothing. Famed British atheist Antony Flew agrees that this is absurd. He shocked the atheist world when he announced in 2004 that he believed in the existence of God. It was the incredible complexity of DNA that opened his eyes. In an interview, Flew stated, "It now seems to me that the findings of more than fifty years of DNA research have provided materials for a new and enormously powerful argument to design," and that he simply "had to go where the evidence leads."[176]

Even the director of the U.S. National Human Genome Research Institute was compelled by the evidence to reason that there is a God. Francis Collins, the scientist who led the team that cracked the human genome, now believes there is a rational basis for a Creator, and that scientific discoveries bring man "closer to God":

> When you have for the first time in front of you this 3.1-billion-letter instruction book that conveys all kinds of information and all kinds of mystery about humankind, you can't survey that going through page after page without a sense of awe. I can't help but look at those pages and have a vague sense that this is giving me a glimpse of God's mind.[177]

Think of the billions of people on the planet, and how each person has his or her own personal DNA. It's not the DNA itself that's so breathtakingly incredible — it's the One who created it and set it in motion.

DNA is not just a book of instructions. It is an actual programming language that instructs the cell's machinery on how to make each unique, specialized cell of your body (in your lungs, kidneys, ears, eyes, etc.) and how it should function.

Try to imagine where you would begin if you had to write a program instructing cells to make the human eye. How would you program it to make the iris, the 137 million light-sensitive cells, the focusing muscles that move 100,000 times a day? Tell it how to communicate with the brain, the blood vessels, the tear ducts, and everything else necessary for sight.

Your Wonderful Body

Think of your body, with its 60,000 miles of blood vessels. In one day, your blood travels 12,000 miles around your body. That's four times the distance across the United States from coast to coast. Think about how nerve impulses travel to and from your brain at speeds up to 250 miles per hour, or how the human brain can read up to 1,000 words per minute. If your brain was a computer, it could perform 38 thousand-trillion operations per second. The world's most powerful supercomputer can manage only .002 percent of that. The human body produces 25 million new cells each second. Every 13 seconds, you produce more cells than there are people in the United States. God made every one of the seven octillion (7,000,000,000,000,000,000,000,00 0,000,000) atoms that make up your body.

We can't begin to understand such creative power. To say that God is absolutely mind-blowingly amazing is infinitely inadequate to a point of absurdity. William Law, a British priest and influential author of the 18th century, wrote:

> What an immense workman is God! In miniature as well as in the great. With the one hand, perhaps, He is making a ring of one hundred thousand miles in diameter, to revolve round a planet like Saturn, and with the other is forming a tooth in the ray of the feather of a hummingbird, or a point in the claw of the foot of a microscopic insect. When He works in miniature, everything is gilded, polished, and perfect, but whatever is made by human art, as a needle, etc., when viewed by a microscope, appears rough, coarse, and bungling.[178]

Past generations had the excuse of ignorance when it came to the instruction book of life. They didn't understand how phenomenally complex even the "simple" cell is. If we could throw off the shackles of an almost contemptuous familiarity when it comes to our eyes, our ears, etc., we could get a glimpse of the power of the One who brought all things into existence.

But the proud and unreasonable atheist believes the absurdity that the universe possessed the ability to make itself, before it existed. It wasn't; then suddenly, it just was — and they believe nothing caused it. If you find that hard to believe, watch our movie *The Atheist Delusion* (TheAtheistDelusion.com) and see the pied piper of atheism, Richard Dawkins, espousing his belief that nothing created everything, making himself look foolish as he does so.

The third reason atheists aren't trusted with high political office is that they (by definition) are foolish. While many deny it, because it's an intellectual embarrassment, they believe the scientific impossibility that nothing created everything. The existence of God can be proven reasonably, simply, and scientifically — to those who are reasonable.

In light of these thoughts, it's understandable why the Founding Fathers believed in God, and why there has never been a U.S. president who professed to be an atheist. It's also clear why Sir Isaac Newton said atheism is "odious" and that atheists are idolaters with their own erroneous image of God. The atheists' issue isn't theological; it's moral — they don't want to believe in an Almighty God to whom they are held accountable. They want to be free to do as they please and engage in whatever sinful pleasures make them happy, without any sense of guilt. Because they don't want to be reminded of a God who sees — and will judge — their every thought and action, they "hate God without a cause" and rail against Christians and Christianity in an effort to make ours a godless society.

So why do Americans, for the most part, not trust an atheist to be a good president of these United States? Atheists, like the rest of us, are not morally "good." Without an unwavering moral compass to guide him, an atheist president would be easily swayed by the winds of popular opinion and his own selfish desires — doing whatever was right in his own eyes. Without a proper fear of God (which the Bible says is "the beginning of wisdom") and an awareness of a coming Day of Judgment, he will no doubt lead the nation further into the dark chasm of moral decadence.

Being the leader of the free world, of "one nation under God," requires incredible wisdom, yet the atheist foolishly rejects the evidence of a Creator that is all around him. Denying his God-given common sense, he thinks the DNA that shapes who he is — that amazingly complex book of life — assembled itself by pure random chance. It's obvious why the Bible calls an atheist a "fool." And so it makes sense as to why so many Americans don't want a fool representing them as the president.

For now, voters will continue to battle between the donkeys and the elephants to rule our land. Until pigs fly over the White House, there will never be an atheist as the U.S. president. So help us God.

Notes

1. Carlos S. Moreno, "An Atheist for Congress?" CNN Opinion, September 1, 2014, <tinyurl.com/jocaz46>.
2. Nick Wing, "Here Are All the Atheists in Congress," *Huffington Post*, Sept. 19, 2013, <tinyurl.com/ly6eddk>.
3. Hemant Mehta, "Former Congressman Barney Frank: 'I Am Not an Atheist,' " March 13, 2015, <tinyurl.com/h8vkxpo>.
4. "Bernie Sanders," Celeb Atheists <tinyurl.com/jg3h8ff>.
5. Frances Stead Sellers and John Wagner, "Why Bernie Sanders doesn't participate in organized religion," *The Washington Post*, Jan. 27, 2016.
6. Kimberly Winston, "Bernie Sanders disappoints some atheists with his 'very strong religious' feelings," Religion News Service, Feb. 4, 2016, <tinyurl.com/jhsvn8n>.
7. Tim Dickinson, "Bernie Sanders' Political Revolution," *Rolling Stone*, November 18, 2015, <tinyurl.com/ntameym>.
8. Jack Jenkins, "Why All of the Atheists in Congress Are Closeted," ThinkProgress, Aug. 26, 2014, <tinyurl.com/jpfxkdy>.
9. Gary Scott Smith, "Americans are deeply religious, so will we ever see an atheist president?" *The Washington Post*, March 23, 2015, <tinyurl.com/gn5dbru>.
10. Jack Jenkins, "Why All of the Atheists in Congress Are Closeted."
11. Gary Scott Smith, "Americans are deeply religious. . . ."
12. Ibid.
13. Hans Villarica, "Study of the Day: Religious People Distrust Atheists as Much as Rapists," *The Atlantic*, Dec. 19, 2011, <tinyurl.com/jjeh3to>.
14. Peter Yeung, "Anti-atheist distrust 'deeply and culturally ingrained,' study finds," *The Independent*, March 25, 2016, <tinyurl.com/hxxrnjn>.

15. Daisy Grewal, "In Atheists We Distrust," *Scientific American*, January 17, 2012, <tinyurl.com/qenl7my>.

16. Trevor Grundy, "Richard Dawkins Pedophilia Remarks Provoke Outrage," Sept. 9, 2013, *Huffington Post*, <tinyurl.com/kqdl6gz>.

17. American Atheists, <tinyurl.com/j3o87p7>.

18. "America's Changing Religious Landscape," Pew Research Center, May 12, 2015, <tinyurl.com/ldnxabw>.

19. Gregory Paul and Phil Zuckerman, "Why do Americans still dislike atheists?" *The Washington Post*, April 29, 2011, <tinyurl.com/z3bkt39>.

20. Vlad Chituc, "CNN Thinks Atheists Are the Devil," *The Daily Beast*, Mar. 25, 2015, <http://thebea.st/1Bq-7JXm>.

21. *The Papers of James Madison*, Robert Rutland, ed. (Chicago, IL: Univ. of Chicago Press, 1973), Vol. 8, p. 299, 304, June 20, 1785.

22. John Witherspoon, *The Works of the Reverend John Witherspoon* (Philadelphia, PA: William W. Woodward, 1802), Vol. III, p. 42.

23. John Jay, *The Correspondence and Public Papers of John Jay*, Henry P. Johnston, ed. (New York: G.P. Putnam's Sons, 1890–93), Vol. 4, p. 365, <oll.libertyfund.org/titles/2330>.

24. Noah Webster, *Letters to a Young Gentleman Commencing His Education* (New Haven, CT: Howe & Spalding, 1823), p. 18–19.

25. "U.S. Public Becoming Less Religious," Pew Research Center, November 3, 2015, <tinyurl.com/pcyjbot>.

26. <tinyurl.com/8t3wny>.

27. <tinyurl.com/htwcurz>.

28. <tinyurl.com/zuues32>.

29. <tinyurl.com/jrsoot6>.

30. <tinyurl.com/mmdumjq>.

31. <tinyurl.com/zjqo6o8>.

32. <tinyurl.com/jc7r9jx>.

33. <tinyurl.com/gv7qoab>.
34. <tinyurl.com/gtmhd9j>.
35. <tinyurl.com/4yyqk3e>.
36. <tinyurl.com/zeaqvtl>.
37. <tinyurl.com/zfldffs>.
38. <tinyurl.com/zfqnhpy>.
39. <tinyurl.com/jxyxqmp>.
40. <tinyurl.com/ojh3szc>.
41. <tinyurl.com/hro2k4v>.
42. <tinyurl.com/jcertea>.
43. <tinyurl.com/h3qrelh>.
44. <tinyurl.com/jngf7ve>.
45. <tinyurl.com/o4x3ral>.
46. <tinyurl.com/h3ethpk>.
47. <tinyurl.com/zuxekbw>.
48. <tinyurl.com/nehkplp>
49. <www.catholic.org/news/national/story.php?id=65901>.
50. <tinyurl.com/j8umk3n>.
51. <tinyurl.com/hdnd78c>.
52. <tinyurl.com/he9au67>.
53. <articles.latimes.com/2008/dec/14/nation/na-weddings14>.
54. <tinyurl.com/j7wjqsq>.
55. <tinyurl.com/hoqc86x>.
56. <tinyurl.com/hcgrgcp>.
57. <tinyurl.com/zej7nue>.
58. <tinyurl.com/z8aby2b>.
59. <tinyurl.com/zbqk4gu>.
60. <tinyurl.com/ju3kvh5>.
61. <atheists.org/legal/current/oklahoma>.
62. <tinyurl.com/h2xzjkh>.
63. <www.sacbee.com/news/local/crime/article2768782.html>.

64. <tinyurl.com/z5ntmry>.
65. <tinyurl.com/zh2blcc>.
66. <tinyurl.com/mjpfzz5>
67. <tinyurl.com/nkrm56v>.
68. <tinyurl.com/jagckgx>.
69. <www.skepticfiles.org/atheist/gideonff.htm>.
70. <tinyurl.com/jjlpzbc>.
71. <tinyurl.com/jlwnytx>.
72. <tinyurl.com/jjfja65>.
73. <tinyurl.com/h4gob8d>.
74. <tinyurl.com/z2wlmux>.
75. <tinyurl.com/j5v7qfm>.
76. <tinyurl.com/zhxhfec>.
77. <tinyurl.com/hy6hrk5>.
78. <tinyurl.com/zhkszm2>.
79. <tinyurl.com/hzhu4pe>.
80. <tinyurl.com/gl7ca3o>.
81. <tinyurl.com/zrktah4>.
82. <tinyurl.com/jrgpuua>.
83. <tinyurl.com/ht48nzq>.
84. <tinyurl.com/hvgvzsg>.
85. <tinyurl.com/oqcqgqv>
86. <tinyurl.com/zzmwqs5>.
87. <tinyurl.com/jk7clvf>.
88. Gregory Paul and Phil Zuckerman, "Why do Americans still dislike atheists?" *The Washington Post*, April 29, 2011, <tinyurl.com/z3bkt39>.
89. Phil Zuckerman, "Why Americans Hate Atheists," *Psychology Today*, June 23, 2014, <tinyurl.com/zymqrzd>.
90. Ibid.
91. Husna Haq, "Ted Cruz: Atheists shouldn't be president. Why are they so vilified?" *The Christian Science Monitor*, November 10, 2015, <tinyurl.com/j7wfklb>.
92. Constitution of the United States, <tinyurl.com/yqm97q>.

93. Husna Haq, "Ted Cruz. . . ."
94. "History of 'In God We Trust,'" U.S. Department of the Treasury, <tinyurl.com/hpw9vul>.
95. Richard Dawkins, in an interview with *The Times of London*, April 2010.
96. "Sharia," Wikipedia, <https://en.wikipedia.org/wiki/Sharia>.
97. Samira Shackle, "There are two places for an atheist in sharia communities: the closet or the grave," *New Humanist*, August 27, 2014, <tinyurl.com/q6x4l5c>.
98. Paul Fidalgo, "Gallup: Record number of Americans would vote for an atheist president," CNN, June 25, 2015, <www.cnn.com/2015/06/25/living/atheist-president-gallup>.
99. Ibid.
100. Cathy Lynn Grossman, "Atheists politicians might be rare now, but not for long," June 29, 2015, <tinyurl.com/zd8b74w>.
101. Ibid.
102. Gary Scott Smith, "Americans are deeply religious, so will we ever see an atheist president?" *The Washington Post*, March 23, 2015, <tinyurl.com/gn5dbru>.
103. Nick Wing, "Ted Cruz: An Atheist 'Isn't Fit To Be' President," *Huffington Post*, Nov. 9, 2015, <tinyurl.com/zkahefv>.
104. Michael Gryboski, "Is Donald Trump an Atheist?" *Christian Post*, March 4, 2016, <tinyurl.com/jgl59vo>.
105. Bryan York, "Dissing McCain not Trump's big problem in Iowa," *Washington Examiner*, July 20, 2015, <tinyurl.com/q8kly9c>.
106. Daniel Silliman, "Hillary Clinton showed up for church today. Will faith help or hurt her on the campaign?" *Washington Post*, September 13, 2015, <tinyurl.com/jl4qt3n>.
107. Stoyan Zaimov, "Bill Maher Says Obama Is Really an Atheist, Mocks Hillary Clinton's Devotion to the Bible," *Christian Post*, June 24, 2014, <tinyurl.com/zl94ze9>.

108. "Jesse Ventura," Wikipedia, <tinyurl.com/huzc96y>.

109. Penn Jillette, "Have Faith, We'll Have an Atheist President," *The New York Times,* March 24, 2015, <tinyurl.com/n6qjhwr>.

110. Ibid.

111. Ibid.

112. Gary Scott Smith, "Americans are deeply religious. . . ."

113. Declaration of Independence, <tinyurl.com/3padsj>.

114. Thomas Jefferson, *Notes on the State of Virginia* (Trenton: Wilson & Blackwell, 1803), Query XVIII, p. 272, <www.pbs.org/jefferson/archives/documents/frame_ih198145.htm>.

115. Thomas Jefferson, Letter to Benjamin Rush, April 21, 1803.

116. Abraham Lincoln, Letter published in the *Illinois Gazette,* August 15, 1846.

117. Abraham Lincoln, Message to Congress, December 1, 1862.

118. Abraham Lincoln, Response to a Serenade, November 8, 1864.

119. Abraham Lincoln, Reply to Loyal Colored People of Baltimore upon Presentation of a Bible on September 7, 1864.

120. Abraham Lincoln, *Lincoln Observed: Civil War Dispatches of Noah Brooks,* Michael Burlingame, ed. (Baltmore, MD: The Johns Hopkins University Press, 1998), p. 210.

121. "Presidential Proclamation — National Day of Prayer," April 29, 2011, <tinyurl.com/hezrutm>.

122. George Washington, *The Last Official Address of His Excellency George Washington to the Legislature of the United States* (Hartford, CT: Hudson and Goodwin, 1783), p. 12.

123. George Washington, *The Writings of Washington,* John C. Fitzpatrick, ed. (Washington, DC: Government Printing Office, 1932), Vol. XV, p. 55, from his speech to the Delaware Indian Chiefs on May 12, 1779.

124. George Washington, General Orders, May 2, 1778, <tinyurl.com/z6qa64n>.

125. George Washington, Farewell Address, September 19, 1796, <tinyurl.com/goht9q4>.

126. James Madison, Letter to William Bradford, November 9, 1772, *The Letters and Other Writings of James Madison* (New York: R. Worthington, 1884).

127. James Madison, Letter to Frederick Beasley, November 20, 1825.

128. James Madison, Letter to William Bradford, September 25, 1773, *The Papers of James Madison*, William T. Hutchinson, ed. (Illinois: University of Chicago Press, 1962), Vol. I, p. 96.

129. Steven Shaw, "Top 10: Unknown Atheists," AskMen.com, <tinyurl.com/zdel3m2>.

130. Benjamin Franklin, *The Writings of Benjamin Franklin*, Vol. 2, Albert Henry Smyth, ed. (New York: The MacMillan Company, 1905), p. 99–100.

131. Benjamin Franklin, Speech to the Constitutional Convention, June 28, 1787, Library of Congress, <tinyurl.com/hwfaw2h>.

132. Benjamin Franklin, *Works of Benjamin Franklin*, John Bigelow, ed. (New York: G.P. Putnam's Sons, 1904), p. 185, to Ezra Stiles, March 9, 1790.

133. "Our founding fathers were not Christians," July 5, 2011, <www.freethought.mbdojo.com/foundingfathers.html>.

134. Michael Lipka, "7 Facts About Atheists," November 5, 2015, Pew Research Center, <tinyurl.com/nofpexk>.

135. <www.pinterest.com/pin/505036545685361092/>.

136. <tinyurl.com/juwnl7p>.

137. "Ray Comfort claims to find a Cure for Cancer," *Canterbury Atheist*, March 23, 2009, <tinyurl.com/h5u4lzu>.

138. See www.audacitymovie.com.

139. "Audacity," User Ratings, IMBd, <tinyurl.com/nssyhxg>.

140. Joanna Walters, " 'Good without God': Nebraska atheists take over nativity to promote tolerance," *The Guardian*, Dec. 12, 2015, <tinyurl.com/pu34w34>.

141. Daniel White, "Atheist 'Nativity' Scene Removed from Texas State Capitol for 'Mocking' Christians," Time, Dec. 23, 2015, <time.com/4160737/mock-nativity-texas-capitol>.

142. Amanda Marcotte, "The 8 most atheist-friendly countries in the world," Salon, Aug. 17, 2015, <tinyurl.com/z6q6evo>.

143. Gary Scott Smith, "Americans are deeply religious. . . ."

144. "The happiest countries are also the least religious," <tinyurl.com/jny3nvp>.

145. Phil Zuckerman, "Atheism: Contemporary Rates and Patterns," *Cambridge Companion to Atheism*, Michael Martin, ed. (New York: University of Cambridge Press, 2007), <tinyurl.com/pkzcmvu, p. 5>.

146. "Losing our religion? Two thirds of people still claim to be religious," Gallup, April 13, 2015, <tinyurl.com/ja37yps>.

147. "Numbers of Atheists by country during 2005 and 2012," Religious Tolerance, <tinyurl.com/hck5wep>.

148. Charlotte Celsing, "Are Swedes losing their religion?" Sept. 1, 2006, <https://archive.is/PTcF>.

149. Peter Steinfels, "Scandinavian Nonbelievers, Which Is Not to Say Atheists," *The New York Times*, Feb. 27, 2009, <www.nytimes.com/2009/02/28/us/28beliefs.html>.

150. Ibid.

151. Bojan Milosevic, "11 Countries with Highest Atheist Population," October 11, 2015, <tinyurl.com/hudo324>.

152. "Benito Mussolini," More or Less: Heroes and Killers of the 20th Century, <tinyurl.com/jkzaenl>.

153. "Death of Benito Mussolini," <tinyurl.com/h3x6r44>.

154. Tim Stanley, "The Left is trying to rehabilitate Karl Marx. Let's remind them of the millions who died in

his name," *The Telegraph,* November 1, 2013, <tinyurl.com/klqzzfe>.

155. Palash Ghosh, "How Many People Did Joseph Stalin Kill?" *International Business Times,* March 5, 2013, <www.ibtimes.com/how-many-people-did-joseph-stalin-kill-1111789>.

156. Juan Carlos Escoriaza, "Top Ten Most Evil Dictators of All Time," May 4, 2010, PopTen, <tinyurl.com/7cynlog>.

157. "Vladimir Ilyich Lenin," More or Less: Heroes and Killers of the 20th Century, <tinyurl.com/j6kwcnd>.

158. R.J. Rummel, *Death by Government* (New Brunswick, NJ: Transaction Publishers, 1994), <tinyurl.com/y4ne3n>.

159. Vox Day, *The Irrational Atheist: Dissecting the Unholy Trinity of Dawkins, Harris, and Hitchens* (Dallas, TX: BenBella Books, Inc., 2008), p. 240.

160. Charles Phillips and Alan Axelrod, *Encyclopedia of Wars* (New York: Fact on File, Inc., 2005).

161. Rick Noack, "These Are the World's Least Religious Countries," *The Washington Post,* April 14, 2015, <tinyurl.com/pkxxtdq>.

162. "Cracks in the atheist edifice," *The Economist,* Nov. 1, 2014, <tinyurl.com/oerakqy>.

163. Ibid.

164. Jerry A. Coyne, "As atheists know, you can be good without God," *USA Today,* Aug. 1, 2011, <tinyurl.com/kts23ek>.

165. Ronald A. Lindsay, "Good Without God — But Better Without God?" *Secular Humanism,* July 17, 2015, <tinyurl.com/zvbxz96>.

166. Holly Meyer, "Atheists, non-religious talk morality, secular issues in Nashville," *The Tennessean,* March 5, 2016, <tinyurl.com/z5867rm>.

167. God commands all believers to be baptized and become a committed part of a local Christian church. See

"Save Yourself Some Pain" on LivingWaters.com to learn more.

168. Jill Meadows, letter to the editor, *The Des Moines Register*, January 5, 2016, <tinyurl.com/zlbjaht>.

169. Ravi Somaiya, "Sean Penn Met With 'El Chapo' for Interview in His Hide-Out," *The New York Times*, Jan. 9, 2016, <tinyurl.com/h3eof5n>.

170. Sean Penn, "El Chapo Speaks," *Rolling Stone*, January 9, 2016, <tinyurl.com/h7mrrfz>.

171. Richard Dawkins, *The God Delusion* (New York: Houghton Mifflin, 2008), p. 51.

172. Michael Denton, *Evolution: A Theory in Crisis* (Bethesda, MD: Adler & Adler, 1986), p. 250.

173. Charles B. Thaxton, Ph.D., "DNA, Design and the Origin of Life," November 13–16, 1986, <tinyurl.com/jvf82qo>.

174. Elizabeth Sheldon, "How Is a Cell's DNA Like the Books in a Library?" The Classroom, <tinyurl.com/hgl345r>.

175. Ibid.

176. Rich Deem, "One Flew Over the Cuckoo's Nest?" <www.godandscience.org/apologetics/flew.html>.

177. Steven Swinford, "I've found God, says man who cracked the genome," June 11, 2006, <tinyurl.com/5ltzda>.

178. *The Saturday Magazine*, Vol. 1 (London: John William Parker, 1832), p. 111.

Resources

If you have not yet placed your trust in Jesus Christ and would like additional information, please visit LivingWaters.com and check out the following helpful resources:

The Evidence Bible. Answers to over 200 questions, thousands of comments, and over 130 informative articles will help you better comprehend the Christian faith.

How to Know God Exists: Scientific Proof of God. Clear evidences for His existence will convince you that belief in God is reasonable and rational — a matter of fact and not faith.

Why Christianity? (DVD). If you have ever asked what happens after we die, if there is a heaven, or how good we have to be to go there, this DVD will help you.

If you are a new believer, please read Save Yourself Some Pain, written just for you (available free online at LivingWaters.com, or as a booklet).

For Christians

Please visit our website where you can sign up for our free weekly e-newsletter. To learn how to share your faith the way Jesus did, don't miss these helpful resources:

God Has a Wonderful Plan for Your Life: The Myth of the Modern Message (our most important book). This essential teaching, in a brief, easy-to-read book, is designed for anyone who wants to quickly learn how to share the gospel biblically.

Hell's Best Kept Secret and True & False Conversion. Listen to these vital messages free at LivingWaters.com.

How to Bring Your Children to Christ ... & Keep Them There. These time-tested principles will help you guide your children to experience genuine salvation and avoid the pitfall of rebellion.